A BIG STINK

A BIG STINK

A Tale of Ardor and Odor

EDWARD H. KAFKA-GELBRECHT
Renowned Scholar of Gastrointestinal Humor

ILLUSTRATIONS BY SOPHIA VINCENT GUY

TEN SPEED PRESS
California | New York

For E & Y,
who have always had my back.

Someone did it.
No one will admit it.

Dear Editors,

The Sumerians carved it in stone. The
Romans loved it in Latin. Chaucer let
it loose in Middle English. Shakespeare
refined it and left his audience gasping
in the aisles. Gastrointestinal humor is
as old as civilization itself—the diversion
of kings, the pastime of the rank and file.

I am the author of more than a dozen
academic articles on gastrointestinal
humor. My work plumbs the depths of
anatomy, etymology, volcanology, musicology,
military ordnance, and cheese science.
"Run Silent, Run Deadly"—my explosive
pamphlet on the Soviet submarine mutiny
during the infamous Naval Cabbage Surplus
of 1983—received a starred review in
Intestinal Tracts, the official organ
of the Society of Digestive Literatures.
Perhaps you have encountered my self-
published monograph, "Personal Exhaust"?

My life's work has been to trace each
risible emission to its obscure source. And
yet, too often we scholars busy ourselves
with rearguard actions, stagnating in the
stale air of our ivory towers.

After sifting through centuries of badinage, I believe I have at last succeeded in distilling the essence of one fragrant strain of mirth: I refer to the universal desire to determine the status of the flatus, the owner of the groaner, whom to thank for the "stank"—that is, the need to breezily assert that we, ourselves, are not the author of the cougher.

I submit to your publishing house the first-ever historical account of a crucial moment in the denial of the vile. It has remained a tightly held secret within my family. The time is ripe to give it wide release.

The following tale begins one balmy August afternoon in New York City, many years ago. . . .

Sincerely yours,

Edward H. Kafka-Gelbrecht

"Really, miss."

"Have you considered that
she who denied it, supplied it?"

"Perhaps—but he who noted it, floated it."

"And yet: she who slighted it, ignited it."

"He who disowned it, cologned it."

"She who assumed it, perfumed it."

"He who opposed it, composed it."

"He who impugned it, fine-tuned it."

"She who disputed it, fluted it."

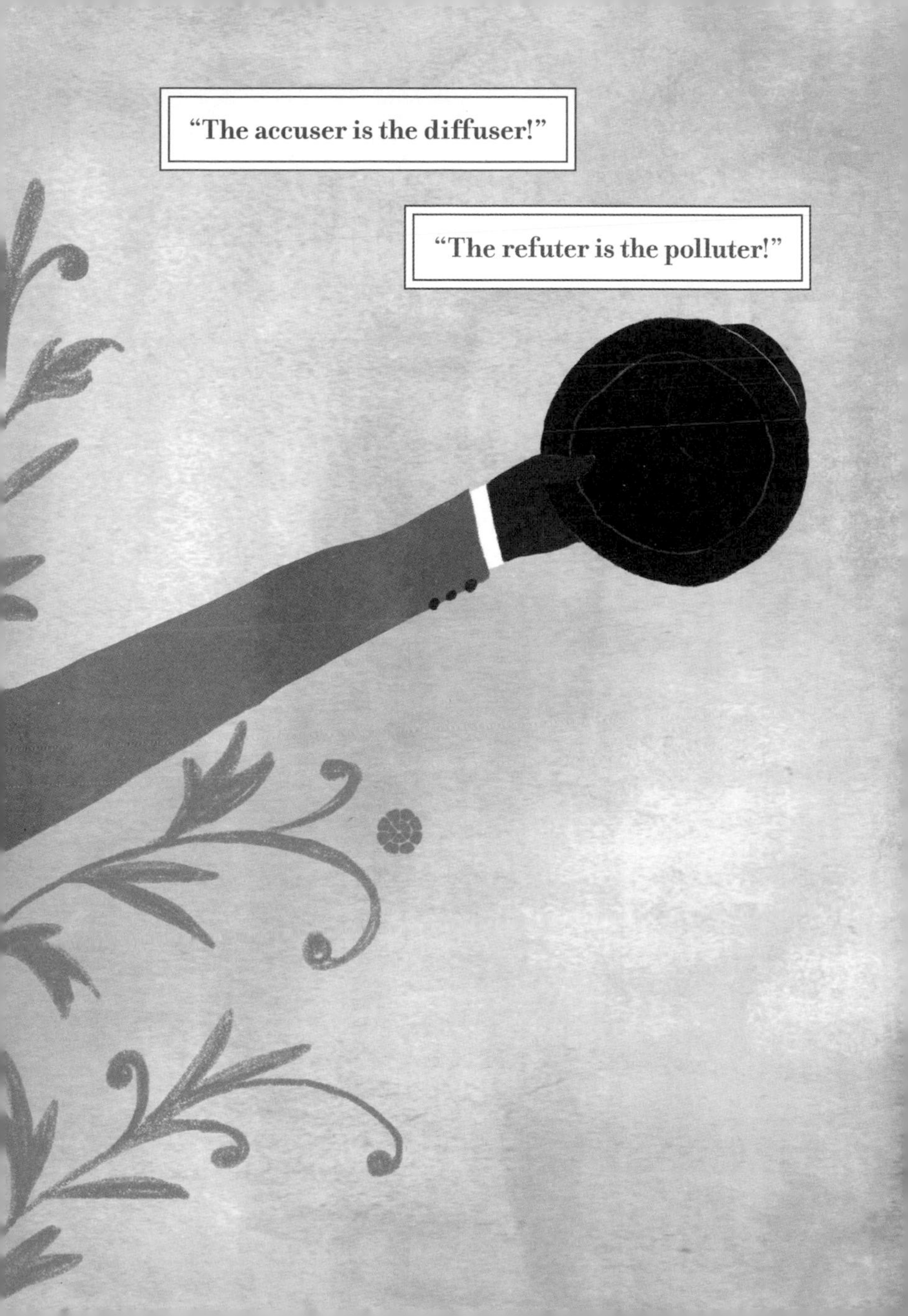
"The accuser is the diffuser!"
"The refuter is the polluter!"

"No need to make a big stink over a little one."

"Abigail Kafka."

"Morris Gelbrecht."

"Well, Mr. Gelbrecht:
he who observed it, served it."

"She who mumbled it, rumbled it!"

"He who explained it, unchained it!"

"While she who depicted it, inflicted it, Miss Kafka."

"But he who found it, unwound it."

Dear Mr. Kafka-Gelbrecht,

Thank you for your recent submission. The manuscript is a bit too brief—or is it a bit too boxers? We also question its relevance to posterity. Might this be little more than a fusty family footnote? Does today's reader savor this sort of pungent back and forth? We think our audience will pass. Sorry to deflate you, but so must we.

Sincerely,

The Editors

Dear Editors,

A mere footnote? Malarkey! These are fundamental questions of groupstink. How does a coworker broker a choker? How do teams of teens esteem their beans?[1] And how do geeks speak of reeks for weeks?

I did not send the following materials earlier as I did not wish to suffocate you with evidence. Enclosed is my back catalog—the results of a decade of dogged fieldwork, conducted at great olfactory discomfort.

The world is a fog of confusion, dear editors. I believe the fruits of my research will buttress my argument: we are all searching for odor in disorder.

Yours with bated breath,

Edward H. Kafka-Gelbrecht

1 See Kittridge's work on Connecticut JV lacrosse in *Social Miasmas*, 15(3):619–639.

"She who scented it, vented it."

"He who nixed it, mixed it."

"She who unmasked it, unflasked it."

"He who excluded it, extruded it."

"She who cursed it, dispersed it."
"She who foreswore it, tore it."
"She who spoke the sin, broke the wind."

"He who thunk it, stunk it."
"He who catched it, hatched it."
"He who narc'd it, sparked it."
TOO LOUD? TOO BAD!

"He who tweeted it, heated it."

"He who cawed it, thawed it."

"She who IDed, freed it."

"He who downplayed it, laid it."

"He who suggested it, un-nested it."

"She who mocked it, squawked it."

"He who pooh-poohed it, cuckooed it."

"She who pursued it, *tu-whit-tu-who*'d it."

"He who chirped it, bottom-burped it."

"She who betrayed it, sautéed it."
"He who eschewed it, home-brewed it!"
"She who denied it, deep-fried it."

"He who faked it, baked it."

"She who ghosted it, toasted it."

"He who looked askance, cooked his pants."

"She who perceived it, conceived it!"
"He who disclaimed it, aimed it!"
"He who nosed it, deposed it!"
"She who posited it, deposited it!"
"He who rebutted it . . . butted it!"

Dear Edward,

This is growing stronger—it's quite bracing, in fact.
We are willing to revisit your original submission—
those poor souls in the elevator. However, we wonder:
for all its attention to rear emissions, does the story
have a proper end?

Sincerely,

The Editors

"Do you . . ."

"Not I."

"I deny."

Dear Edward,

May we call you Eddie? This is a fine button on the classic "meet toot"! Did it really happen this way? Does it pass the smell test? Like roses, we say. We'll gladly hold our noses and publish your findings. In fact, we have several sound ideas for the audiobook. We look forward to meeting you in our offices at your earliest convenience.

Yours truly,

The Editors

P.S.: We are on the 18th floor.
Please take the stairs.

ACKNOWLEDGMENTS

Profound thanks to my gutsy literary agent Danielle Svetcov—you vetted the fetid, disputed the putrid, and found the crease through which this book was able to seep out into the world. My deep appreciation also goes out to Sarah Malarkey, editor extraordinaire, who has a nose for refinement.

This book would be stale limburger without the talent and tenacity of Sophia Vincent Guy (if that is her real name), who worked her tail off translating brain-breaking odors into mind-blowing images.

I must also recognize a gaggle of youths (S, A_2, O, N, and R) whose juvenile repartee first showed me how airy banter might yield fragrant insight.

Begrudging gratitude is also due to my rival scholars, who pushed me to apply myself—particularly the early work of Dirk Londonderry (*The Syncopated Belch*) and S. A. Chiswick (*Long Island Colons: Continuity and Change*), as well as Jacee Kessel's photo essay, "Unseen, Unclean." Gentlemen, *now* who's shooting hoops in his own backyard?!

I must also acknowledge Wanda Chang-Diaz's *The People's Guide to Bad Deli and Its Consequences*, with its excellent chapter on slipping, unobserved, out the rear door. Thanks also to Nutz Soda, Dauber's Fast-Acting Melanchthon tablets, Bob the Security Guard, and Randy Katz.

And finally, to my parents: You taught me to hold nothing back, concentrate my efforts, give it my best shot, and, in the end, never be afraid to toot my own horn. Though a long time coming, this pioneering treatise has, I hope, fulfilled your dreams for me. You are the wind beneath my windbreaker.

—EDWARD H. KAFKA-GELBRECHT

A huge thank you to my husband: you patiently and lovingly held down the fort as I holed up in my Mediterranean studio breathing life into 100-year-old wheezes. Thank you to my curious and creative children for filling the studio with fresh smells, bright paintings, and peals of laughter. Thank you to my parents who have supported me through all my adventures—for holding me tightly, for giving me breathing room, for setting me free. Thank you to Dagmar Persson for keeping our egregious effluvia under your hat. Thank you to Sarah Malarkey for offering me first crack at this book, and to Sarah, Danielle Svetcov, and Chloe Rawlins for lighting a fire—it's been a gas! (And Edward, as I've told you many times now: this is my real name.)

— SOPHIA VINCENT GUY

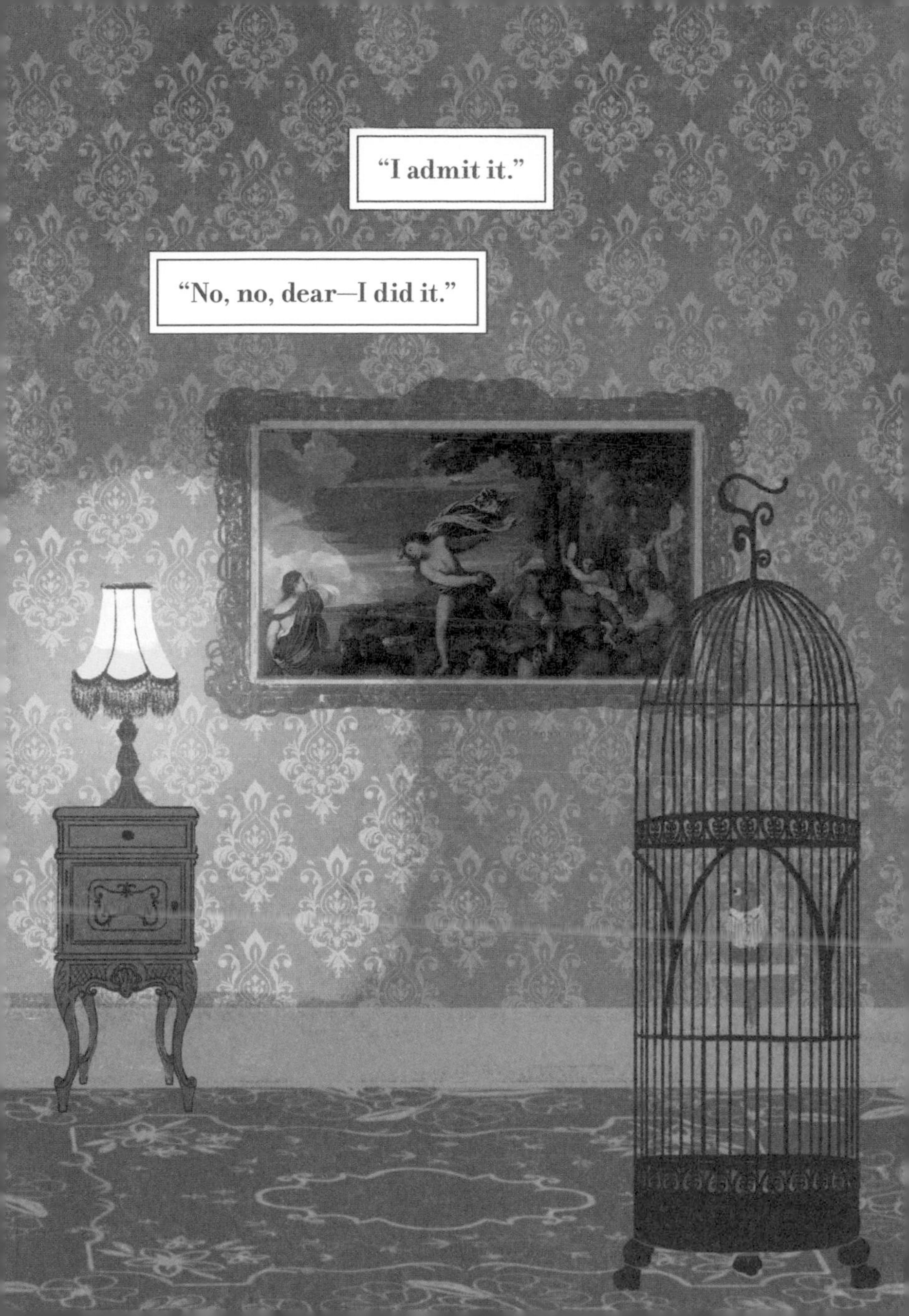
"I admit it."
"No, no, dear—I did it."

Library of Congress Control Number: 2021936795

Hardcover ISBN: 978-1-9848-5957-0
eBook ISBN: 978-1-9848-5958-7

Printed in China

Editor: Sarah Malarkey | Production editor: Kimmy Tejasindhu
Art director and designer: Chloe Rawlins
Production manager: Jane Chinn
Copyeditor: Jennifer Traig | Proofreader: Karen Levy
Publicist: Natalie Yera | Marketer: Daniel Wikey

10 9 8 7 6 5 4 3 2 1

First Edition